MAR 0 8 2016

W9-BQT-046

Dolley Madison

by Amie Jane Leavitt

FIRST LADIES SECOND TO NONE

PURPLE TOAD
PUBLISHING

FIRST LADIES: SECOND TO NONE

Abigail Adams
Dolley Madison
Edith Wilson
Eleanor Roosevelt
Hillary Rodham Clinton
Mary Todd Lincoln

PUBLISHER'S NOTE: The data in this book has been researched in depth, and to the best of our knowledge is factual. Although every measure is taken to give an accurate account, Purple Toad Publishing makes no warranty of the accuracy of the information and is not liable for damages caused by inaccuracies.

Printing 1 2 3 4 5 6 7 8 9

Publisher's Cataloging-in-Publication Data
Leavitt, Amie Jane.
  Dolley Madison / written by Amie Jane Leavitt.
    p. cm.
            Includes bibliographic references and index.
            ISBN 9781624691706
1. Madison, Dolley, 1768-1849--Juvenile literature.
2. Madison, James, 1751-1836--Juvenile literature. 3.
Presidents' spouses--United States--Biography--Juvenile
literature. I. Series: First Ladies : Second to None.
  E342.1 2016
  973.51092
            Library of Congress Control Number: 2015941825

eBook ISBN: 9781624691713

Contents

Chapter One
FIRE IN WASHINGTON

Cannons boomed outside the White House window, startling Dolley Madison out of her brief sleep. She leaped out of bed, grabbed her spyglass, and hurried to the roof.

Dolley could see the battle that had been going on between the American troops and the British Redcoats for days. Even though the cannon fire sounded close, she saw that the fighting was really miles away. Certainly the British would not invade Washington. She believed this even though many Washingtonians had already fled to the neighboring countryside. Even the troops that had been stationed on the White House lawn had retreated. Dolley did not want to abandon her cherished city and the house that she had helped furnish and decorate. She was determined to stay at the White House until her beloved Jimmy, U.S. President James Madison, returned from leading the troops.

Dolley spent the rest of the day going about business as usual. Occasionally, she returned to the roof to check on the battle, but nothing seemed to change. "Surely, James and his men will be back tonight for supper," she thought. She asked the kitchen staff to start cooking his

"The British are coming" may have been a war cry during the Revolutionary War, but it was also a call to arms during the War of 1812. In August 1814, the British invaded the capital city of Washington, D.C.

favorite meal and set the dining room table for 40 guests. Dolley loved entertaining and hoped that by this evening things would finally be back to normal at the White House.

She also kept adding to a letter that she had been writing to her sister. She included entries at noon and at three o'clock. Around the latter time, two messengers rushed into the White House, covered in dust and out of breath. They urged Dolley to depart—it was far too dangerous for her to stay in Washington any longer. Dolley refused. She wanted to wait for James.

Then she remembered what James had told her before he left. "Make sure you gather the state papers and other important things if you need to leave." Dolley made haste. She already had the nation's important papers tucked away into trunks. At this time, she instructed the servants to carry the trunks out to the carriages.

The cannons outside Washington kept on booming—their echoing sounds seemed to grow closer and closer. Shortly after the two messengers left, someone else charged toward the White House. It was the Madisons' good friend Charles Carroll. When he rushed through the door, he was very upset to see Dolley still there. He demanded that she leave with him at once. The British were within a mile of the city. He assured her that they would delight in taking the president's wife captive.

Dolley finally accepted the fact that she had to leave. She dashed through the house gathering anything important she could see. As she hurried past the oval drawing room, she noticed the red velvet curtains. She had adamantly insisted that they be part of the room's décor, and now she couldn't bear to leave them behind. "Take down the curtains," she beseeched the servants.

Dolley Madison leaving the White House

Then she spied the silver service, recently polished and proudly displayed on the cabinet. That simply couldn't be left behind either. She couldn't let the British have such an important and valuable part of the White House. She grabbed as much of it as she could and asked her servants to help her with the rest. Then, as she walked through the dining room, she saw the life-size portrait of George Washington that had been painted by the accomplished artist Gilbert Stuart. Certainly the British would love to parade the portrait of America's first president through the streets of London. No! She would not allow such disrespect to her nation. She implored the servants to remove the painting from the wall.

Gilbert Stuart's painting of George Washington

When they couldn't get it down fast enough, she told them to break the frame. There was no time to carefully take it from the wall and she couldn't leave it behind!

With the portrait out of the frame and securely in a wagon, she sent it on with two friends who were journeying northward. Then she departed with Mr. Carroll in another carriage, with her red velvet curtains, the state papers, and the silver service safely in tow.

As they rushed toward Carroll's Dumbarton home in Georgetown, Dolley looked back to catch a glimpse of the ivory exterior of her cherished White House. Her heart ached to leave the home she had grown to love.

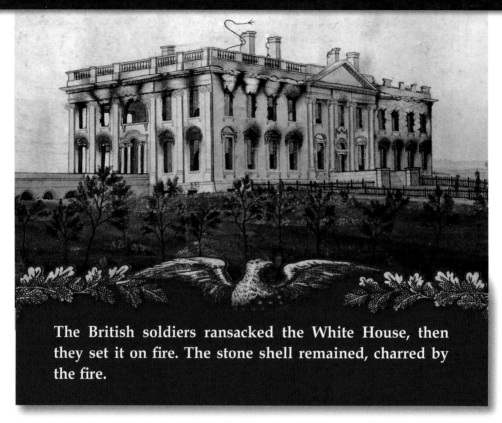

The British soldiers ransacked the White House, then they set it on fire. The stone shell remained, charred by the fire.

Little did she know it would be the last time she would leave the White House. She would never live there again.

Shortly after her flight, the British arrived. They ate the meal she had prepared for James. Then they ransacked the house and set it on fire, just as they had done to the Capitol building shortly before. All of the important buildings in Washington were ablaze. Everything inside the White House was destroyed. The only things left to remind the nation of the early years of the White House were in Dolley's wagons.

But this wasn't the end of the White House. It would be rebuilt after the war, and George Washington's famous portrait, which Dolley had so bravely saved, would once again grace its walls. Because of Dolley's courageous actions on August 24, 1814, her name would forever be memorialized in the pages of American history as a patriot and a heroine.

Dolley's 1814 Letter, Part 1

Dolley wrote a letter to her sister on August 23 and 24, 1814. Here is the first part of the letter, which she wrote on Tuesday, August 23. The second part of the letter, written on Wednesday, August 24, is found in Chapter 4.

Part 1
Tuesday, August 23, 1814

> *Dear Sister,*
> *My husband left me yesterday morning to join Gen. Winder. He enquired anxiously whether I had courage, or firmness to remain in the President's house until his return, on the morrow, or succeeding day, and on my assurance that I had no fear but for him and the success of our army, he left me, beseeching me to take care of myself, and of the cabinet papers, public and private. I have since recd. two dispatches from him, written with a pencil; the last is alarming, because he desires I should be ready at a moment's warning to enter my carriage and leave the city; that the enemy seemed stronger than had been reported, and that it might happen that they would reach the city, with intention to destroy it. . . . I am accordingly ready; I have pressed as many cabinet papers into trunks as to fill one carriage; our private property must be sacrificed, as it is impossible to procure wagons for its transportation. I am determined not to go myself until I see Mr. Madison safe, and he can accompany me, as I hear of much hostility toward him, . . . disaffection stalks around us. . . . My friends and acquaintances are all gone; Even Col. C with his hundred men, who were stationed as a guard in the enclosure. . . . French John (a faithful domestic,) with his usual activity and resolution, offers to spike the cannon at the gate, and to lay a train of powder which would blow up the British, should they enter the house. To the last proposition I positively object, without being able, however, to make him understand why all advantages in war may not be taken.*[1]

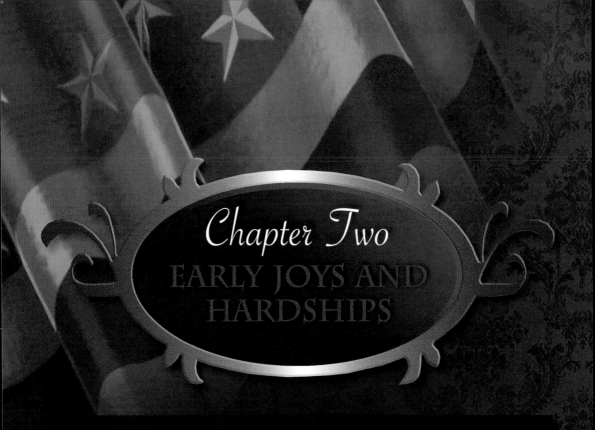

Chapter Two
EARLY JOYS AND HARDSHIPS

In a small town near present-day Greensboro, North Carolina, Dolley Payne was born on May 20, 1768. Her father was John Payne and her mother was Mary Coles Payne. She had four brothers (Walter, William Temple, Isaac, and John) and three sisters (Lucy, Anna, and Mary).

Less than a year after Dolley's birth, the family moved from North Carolina back to Virginia. The Paynes and the Coles had lived in Virginia for generations and were very much part of the colony's important social circles. On the Payne side of the family, Dolley descended from Sir Thomas Fleming, who settled in Virginia shortly after Jamestown was founded.[1] On the Coles side of the family, Dolley was related to Patrick Henry, her mother's first cousin. Dolley's family was also good friends with other noteworthy Virginians.[2] Her mother had even been courted by Thomas Jefferson for a time.[3] Because of all of these familial connections that went back more than 150 years, Dolley always considered herself a Virginian, even though she had been born in North Carolina.

Dolley's family was part of the Quaker faith. Quakers generally wore plain, conservative clothing. Women and girls wore dainty white caps and never wore jewelry or other fancy apparel. This was a little challenging for

Known far and wide for her beauty and her delightful personality, Dolley Madison would be remembered for her courage and grace.

Patrick Henry, the Governor of Virginia, sold his farm named Scotch Town to John Payne for 600 pounds. It was called Scotch Town in colonial days for it was once part of a Scotch settlement.

Dolley because from a young age she had an interest in fashion. When she was a young child, her grandmother gave her some old-fashioned jewelry to play with. Dolley wished she could wear it in public, but knew she wasn't allowed. So, when she went to school, she would wear it in a small cloth bag underneath her clothing. One time when she was playing, the bag broke and the precious jewelry was scattered and lost in the woods.[4] Young Dolley was likely heartbroken over the loss of her special treasure.

In 1775, when Dolley was just seven years old, the first shots of the Revolutionary War rang out at Lexington and Concord in Massachusetts. Even though war boomed on throughout the colonies for eight years, Dolley's childhood was relatively peaceful. She grew up on a large plantation in Hanover County, Virginia.

Plantations needed hundreds of workers to run smoothly. Workers planted and harvested the crops in the fields. They took care of the animals. They made tools and furniture and cooked the food. In the 1700s, plantation workers were generally people from Africa who had been taken as slaves. Dolley's father, John Payne, owned many slaves on his plantation. However, his Quaker beliefs convinced him that slavery was wrong. He eventually made a critical decision. In 1783, after the end of the Revolutionary War, he freed all of his slaves. This decision ended his life as a planter. He sold his plantation and moved his family 200 miles north to the city of Philadelphia.

Philadelphia was an exciting place in the late 1700s. The Paynes had only been in Philadelphia a few years when the delegates from the newly declared states met in 1787 to draft the U.S. Constitution. During the summer and early fall of that year, such noteworthy figures as George Washington, Alexander Hamilton, Benjamin Franklin, and James Madison, who would be known as the Father of the Constitution, were convening daily in Independence Hall.

When the Paynes moved to Philadelphia, Dolley was 15 years old. She was tall and slender. She had an oval face, an ivory complexion, hair as black as raven feathers, and sea-blue eyes. She was indeed very beautiful,

Independence Hall was an important place in colonial Philadelphia. It is where the Declaration of Independence and the U.S. Constitution were signed.

and with her friendly and happy personality, she quickly made many friends.

When Dolley was 22, a young Quaker lawyer named John Todd became interested in her. He asked Dolley's father for permission to marry her. At first, Dolley wasn't interested in the proposal; in fact, she even said that she "never meant to marry."[5] But her father really liked John Todd and felt he would be a good husband for Dolley. Dolley agreed to follow her father's advice, and she married John Todd on January 7, 1790.

The young couple set up their first house in downtown Philadelphia on the corner of 4th and Walnut Streets, just two blocks from Independence Hall.[6] In 1790, Philadelphia had become the nation's capital while Washington, D.C., was being constructed. The city was bustling with congressmen and senators making laws for the new country. John and Dolley lived right in the middle of all the political action. John Todd's law practice was doing well before they wed, and now it really thrived. He set

This house is where Dolley Todd lived when she was first married.

up his office on the first floor of their home and his apprentice, Isaac Heston, lived in a small room in the home's attic.[7] During this time, Dolley's younger sister, Anna, lived with them, too. Dolley became very close to her little sister and often referred to her as her sister-daughter.

The year 1792 was one of big changes for Dolley. On February 29, she gave birth to her first son. She named him John Payne Todd, after her father. Later that year, Dolley's sister Lucy married George Washington's nephew, George Steptoe Washington, and moved to Harewood Plantation in what is now West Virginia. Later that

Anna Payne, shown here, was often called Dolley's sister-daughter because she lived with the Todds when they were first married.

year, Dolley's beloved father passed away, leaving her mother to raise the youngest two children—Mary and John—on her own.

In late 1793, Dolley gave birth to their second son, William Temple Todd, whom she named after her brother. At about that time, a dreaded disease descended upon Philadelphia. At first, people thought it was just a regular sickness, but when more and more people became ill and died with the same symptoms, Dr. Benjamin Rush diagnosed the epidemic as yellow fever. Not much was known about the disease in those days. We know now that it is spread by mosquitoes, but back then, people thought it was spread by human contact. In Philadelphia, people began loading their carts and wagons to leave the city before they or their family members

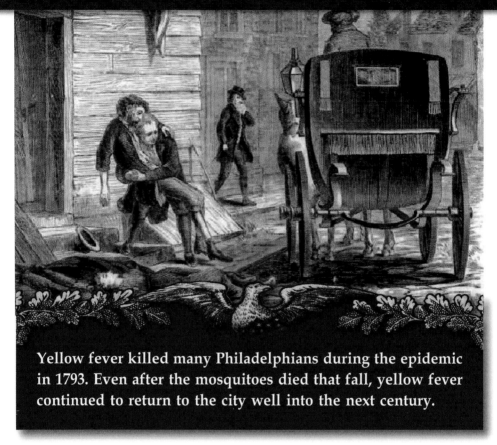

Yellow fever killed many Philadelphians during the epidemic in 1793. Even after the mosquitoes died that fall, yellow fever continued to return to the city well into the next century.

contracted the disease. About half the residents of the city—17,000 people—fled within a matter of weeks.

Dolley was also one of those Philadelphians who escaped the city. John loaded her and their two young sons into a wagon and sent her to the countryside to an area called Grey's Ferry. John promised to join her, but he needed to stay behind to help his parents and his apprentice—they were all sick with the disease and had no one to take care of them. Even though John did his best to nurse them back to health, they did not make it. John, too, contracted the disease. By the time he made it to Grey's Ferry, he was desperately ill. He stumbled into Dolley's waiting arms and died a few hours later.

Dolley hardly had time to grieve the death of her husband before her infant son became ill. Tiny William Temple Todd died just a few days later. The Yellow Fever Epidemic of 1793 took the lives of 5,000 Philadelphians including Dolley's father-in-law, mother-in-law, husband, and baby son. [8]

Thomas Jefferson's Yellow Fever Letter

On September 11, 1793, Thomas Jefferson wrote a letter to Pennsylvania's U.S. Senator, Robert Morris, explaining the dire circumstances in Philadelphia during the yellow fever epidemic:

An infectious and mortal fever is broke out in this place. The deaths under it the week before last were about forty, the last week about fifty, this week they will probably be about two hundreds, and it is increasing. Everyone is getting out of the city who can. Colonel Hamilton is ill of the fever, but is on the recovery. The President [Washington], according to an arrangement of some time ago, set out for Mount Vernon yesterday. The Secretary of War [Henry Knox] is setting out on a visit to Massachusetts. I shall go in a few days to Virginia.[9]

Thomas Jefferson

Chapter Three
MRS. MADISON

By the age of 25, Dolley Payne Todd was already a widow with a two-year-old son to raise on her own. Fortunately for Dolley, John had been successful in his law practice and had amassed enough money and property that she was able to support herself. [1]

Even though Dolley was a widow in mourning, the eligible men of Philadelphia noticed her. She was still beautiful, and as one of her friends observed while she was out on a walk with Dolley, "gentlemen would station themselves [along her path] where they could see her pass." This same friend once also jokingly said, "Really, Dolley, thou must hide thy face, there are so many staring at thee."[2]

One man who took particular notice of Dolley was James Madison, a congressman from Virginia. At 42 years old, he was 17 years older than Dolley and had never been married. As soon as he saw her, he knew he just *had* to meet her. He asked Aaron Burr—an associate who was staying at Dolley's mother's boardinghouse—to set up an introduction. Dolley recorded this experience in a letter to a friend: "Dear friend, thou must come to me. Aaron Burr says that the 'great little Madison' has asked to be

James Madison, who was only 32 years old in 1783, was considered the Father of the Constitution.

brought to me this evening." By the tone of this letter, Dolley was obviously surprised and a little nervous about meeting the famous James Madison. With her concern for fashion, she likely fretted about what to wear and finally decided on a plum-colored satin dress, a dainty tulle kerchief around her neck, and a silk bonnet that framed her face with her jet-black curls. Their first meeting was at her home in May 1794. It was obvious from the start that the two were quite different from each other. Dolley was tall, outgoing, bubbly, and highly social. James was short, shy, studious, and reserved. Despite their differences, they hit it off immediately. James began courting her, and by mid-August 1794, he proposed marriage. Dolley accepted.

As soon as the wedding was announced, it was decided that the couple would be married in Dolley's sister Lucy's home in Virginia. Harewood was a delightful plantation with a rich history. The house was built of blue-gray

The construction of Harewood Mansion was supervised by George Washington.

The beautiful sweeping staircase of Harewood Mansion was the envy of all the plantation owners in the area.

limestone and was known for its magnificent sweeping staircase in the front entryway. George Washington had supervised the construction of the house, which his brother, Samuel, had built in the 1750s. Originally, George Washington had planned to live in the home, but then he inherited Mount Vernon. He spent only some of his winters at Harewood before his brother, Samuel, moved in.[3]

To get to Harewood, Dolley rode with her son, her sister Anna, and a maid in a coach provided by Thomas Jefferson.[4] James and their friends rode beside her in carriages or on horseback. It was about 177 miles from Philadelphia to Harewood. Today, that would take about three hours by car, but by horse and carriage, this journey would have taken many, many days.

Since wedding guests had to travel from such a great distance, they usually stayed at the home for several days—sometimes even a week. Once the bride and groom had arrived at Harewood and all of the guests had been properly rested and settled in at the estate, the ceremony was held. On September 15, 1794, in the parlor of Harewood manor, James and Dolley were married. After the happy couple said their "I do's" and

celebrated in a grand reception with their friends and family, they were showered with rice as they drove off toward Montpelier—James Madison's family plantation in Orange County, Virginia. Dolley was now Dolley Payne Todd Madison, a name she would hold dear for the rest of her life.

Since James was still a member of the House of Representatives, the early years of the Madisons' marriage were spent in Philadelphia. Because she had married James, who was an Episcopalian, Dolley had been read out of the Quaker religion. To be "read out" meant that she was no longer a member of the Quaker faith. It is not known if this was upsetting for Dolley or not, but what is known is that she immediately began embracing the fashions of the day as she likely had always wanted to. From that point on, Dolley Madison was known for her fashionable clothing and distinct sense of style.

Statue of James and Dolley Madison at their home in Montpelier

Dolley was well connected in the high society of the time, both through her own family relations and her husband's. She had been a long time friend of the Washingtons (George and Martha, shown here) as well as other members of the upper crust of the day.

With her marriage to one of the main leaders of the country, Dolley also became much more involved in Philadelphia high society. She was frequently invited to parties—oftentimes to drawing rooms hosted by Martha Washington at the Executive Mansion on the corner of 6th and Market Streets.[5] In the 1700s, a "drawing room" was an informal party or social gathering that was held in the drawing room of a house. At these functions, guests would eat light refreshments, drink punch, and mingle. People could get to know one another in a relaxed and informal way. Dolley grew to love the social scene in Philadelphia. She made many dear friends among the wives of the country's early leaders.

After James finished his term in Congress, he and Dolley moved to Montpelier. They lived there for only a short time, though, before Thomas Jefferson—the third president of the United States—asked James to be his Secretary of State. James accepted the offer and the couple moved back to the capital in 1801, which was now in Washington, D.C.

In 1800, only the north wing of the Capitol was complete. It housed the Congress, the Supreme Court, and the Library of Congress.

Washington City, as it was called then, was a primitive town in the early 1800s. Only 5,000 people called it home, whereas Philadelphia had about 40,000 residents. There were very few buildings, and the dirt roads were often rivers of mud. At first, Dolley was not very happy in her new surroundings, but she made the best of it.

President Jefferson was a widower; his wife had died years before. Because he had never remarried, he needed someone to help host social gatherings, dinners, and other such functions at the White House. His daughter lived too far away, so he would often ask Dolley, or her sister Anna, to help him. As hostess, Dolley became quite well known in Washington among the political leaders and visiting dignitaries.

Dolley was always a champion of good causes. In 1803, President Jefferson was sending Meriwether Lewis and William Clark on an expedition to explore the newly purchased Louisiana Territory. The wives of Jefferson's cabinet members, and especially Dolley, were quite concerned about the dangers these men would face. Dolley spearheaded a fundraising effort to help provide the men and their team with the supplies they would need for their long and difficult journey. She and many of the women of Washington City also donated many necessary items for Lewis and Clark to take with them on their now-famous expedition across the continent.[6]

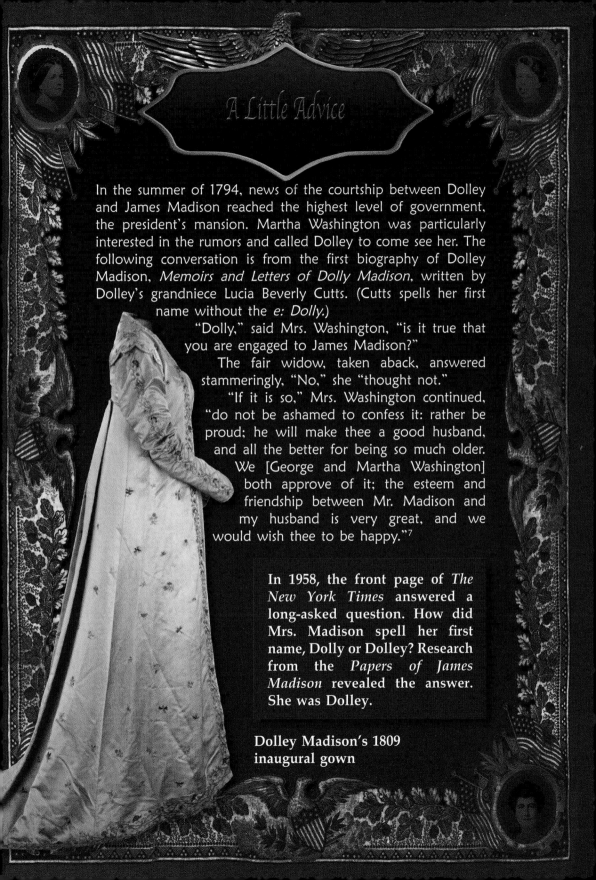

A Little Advice

In the summer of 1794, news of the courtship between Dolley and James Madison reached the highest level of government, the president's mansion. Martha Washington was particularly interested in the rumors and called Dolley to come see her. The following conversation is from the first biography of Dolley Madison, *Memoirs and Letters of Dolly Madison*, written by Dolley's grandniece Lucia Beverly Cutts. (Cutts spells her first name without the *e: Dolly.*)

"Dolly," said Mrs. Washington, "is it true that you are engaged to James Madison?"

The fair widow, taken aback, answered stammeringly, "No," she "thought not."

"If it is so," Mrs. Washington continued, "do not be ashamed to confess it: rather be proud; he will make thee a good husband, and all the better for being so much older. We [George and Martha Washington] both approve of it; the esteem and friendship between Mr. Madison and my husband is very great, and we would wish thee to be happy."[7]

In 1958, the front page of *The New York Times* answered a long-asked question. How did Mrs. Madison spell her first name, Dolly or Dolley? Research from the *Papers of James Madison* revealed the answer. She was Dolley.

Dolley Madison's 1809 inaugural gown

Chapter Four
LIFE AT THE
WHITE HOUSE

In 1808, James Madison was elected the fourth president of the United States. On the evening of the Inauguration, March 4, 1809, Dolley hosted an inaugural ball. Four hundred people came and bought tickets at $4 each (about $78 in today's money).[1] The evening was a huge success. A newspaper from the time period, the *National Intelligencer,* called it the most "brilliant and crowded [event] ever known in Washington." This gala began the tradition of the Inaugural Ball, and every president since James Madison has hosted one.[2]

Dolley chose her outfit for the evening very carefully. She wanted to look regal, but not royal. She was, after all, the wife of the President of the United States; but she did not want to look like she was trying to be the wife of a king! She chose an ivory colored dress made of soft flowing velvet. It had a high empire waist, a scooped neckline, and a long tapered train. Instead of a diamond necklace as royals would have worn, Dolley wore a single strand of pearls with matching earrings and bracelet. Her hair was pulled up, and her delicate black ringlets bounced around her face. A white satin turban sprouted tall feather plumes.

Dolley's ball was the beginning of a long legacy of Inaugural Balls that continues today.

Benjamin Henry Latrobe

When the Madisons moved into the White House, they realized they had their work cut out for them in order to make this a house fit for the president. The two presidents who had lived there previously—Adams and Jefferson—had brought their own furniture with them. When they left office, they naturally took it with them. Dolley felt that the president's home should be furnished with things that stayed permanently and didn't leave at the end of each administration. She asked Congress to give her some money to decorate. They gave her $12,000, which in today's money would be $235,000.[3] She hired architect Benjamin Henry Latrobe and his wife, Mary, to help her. Dolley played a major role in the decisions that were made. For example, at one point Mr. Latrobe and Dolley each had different views on the types of curtains that should be hung in the oval drawing room. Dolley's choice of red velvet won out. Dolley also felt that the furniture should be made in America and have a simple yet elegant feel to it.

As soon as the White House was furnished, Dolley began hosting drawing rooms, political dinners, and public receptions. During Jefferson's administration, the president held separate functions for each political party, not wanting rivals to mingle with each other. But Dolley had a different approach. She felt that social gatherings were a good opportunity for the political leaders to learn how to get along. Tensions were often high in Congress. Sometimes the men got in shouting matches with each other. Sometimes they beat each other with their fists and canes. When tensions really flared, they even challenged each other to duels. At Dolley's parties, the men could meet on more relaxing terms, and would be able to get to know each other. Dolley had a real knack for making people feel at ease. People who knew her said that she never forgot a face, a name, or any of the pertinent details about the people she met. Because of the delightful atmosphere at her parties, everyone in Washington City wanted to attend. Her Wednesday evening drawing room parties were so well attended that they became known as "squeezes" because the room would be so crowded.

Dolley was a natural hostess.

In 1812, Dolley hosted the first wedding ever held at the White House. A few years earlier, George Steptoe Washington passed away, leaving her sister Lucy a widow. Dolley hosted Lucy's wedding to her second husband, Associate Supreme Court Justice Thomas Todd. Not much is recorded about this first White House wedding, but it was likely a delightful event.

Life wasn't all fun and games during James Madison's presidency. From the beginning, the nation had been experiencing difficult relations with Great Britain. Great Britain was at war with France, and the British believed that the United States should be involved, too. When American sailors and merchants were out at sea, British military vessels would commandeer their ships and force the sailors to join the British army. The United States declared war with Great Britain to stop them. This "Second War for Independence" became known as the War of 1812.

Few people believed that the British would actually invade Washington, but in August 1814, the battles drew closer. President Madison briefly left the city to discuss strategy with his generals. Dolley vowed to stay at the White House. When the British were less than a mile away, she simply had to leave.

The White House was nearly completely destroyed by the British. All the work that Dolley had done literally went up in flames.

The flames from the burning White House could be seen from many miles away. It was a devastating sight.

Many people thought that Washington was too far gone to be saved, and that the capital should be moved to another city. Dolley disagreed. As soon as she and James could safely return to the city, they did. They set up residence at a home called the Octagon House, where Dolley immediately began hosting parties. She wanted to show Congress, the country, and the rest of the world that it was business as usual in Washington. Her message was heard loud and clear. Congress voted to keep the capital city in Washington and to start rebuilding.

The Madisons would never live in the White House again—it wasn't rebuilt until James Monroe's presidency. Yet we can definitely thank Dolley for saving two Washingtons for the nation in 1814: the portrait of George Washington now hangs proudly in the White House, and the city of Washington, D.C., is a beautiful and productive capital.

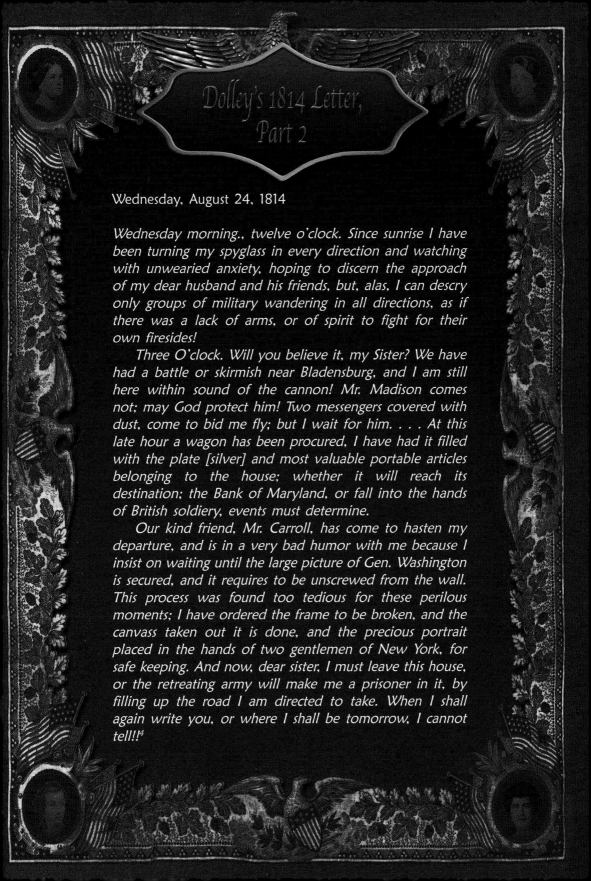

Dolley's 1814 Letter, Part 2

Wednesday, August 24, 1814

Wednesday morning., twelve o'clock. Since sunrise I have been turning my spyglass in every direction and watching with unwearied anxiety, hoping to discern the approach of my dear husband and his friends, but, alas, I can descry only groups of military wandering in all directions, as if there was a lack of arms, or of spirit to fight for their own firesides!

Three O'clock. Will you believe it, my Sister? We have had a battle or skirmish near Bladensburg, and I am still here within sound of the cannon! Mr. Madison comes not; may God protect him! Two messengers covered with dust, come to bid me fly; but I wait for him. . . . At this late hour a wagon has been procured, I have had it filled with the plate [silver] and most valuable portable articles belonging to the house; whether it will reach its destination; the Bank of Maryland, or fall into the hands of British soldiery, events must determine.

Our kind friend, Mr. Carroll, has come to hasten my departure, and is in a very bad humor with me because I insist on waiting until the large picture of Gen. Washington is secured, and it requires to be unscrewed from the wall. This process was found too tedious for these perilous moments; I have ordered the frame to be broken, and the canvass taken out it is done, and the precious portrait placed in the hands of two gentlemen of New York, for safe keeping. And now, dear sister, I must leave this house, or the retreating army will make me a prisoner in it, by filling up the road I am directed to take. When I shall again write you, or where I shall be tomorrow, I cannot tell!![4]

Chapter Five
FIRST
"FIRST LADY"

James Madison served two terms as president. When James Monroe was elected the fifth president, the Madisons returned to Montpelier. James spent his retirement preparing his papers for publication. Dolley rarely left his side during that twenty-year time period. She often served as his secretary and would help him by scribing and editing. Some of the most important papers that they worked on were the detailed daily notes that James had taken as secretary of the Constitutional Convention. Both James and Dolley knew that this information would be invaluable to the history of the country.

Staying at Montpelier proved to be challenging for Dolley. She missed the social scene and excitement of her treasured Washington. She missed the parties, the fashion, and the political drama of the capital. She kept up on it the best she could by corresponding with her friends in the city.

On the other hand, Dolley never regretted the time she spent with her dear husband. During the last few years of his life, he needed a great deal of help and Dolley was constantly by his side. James Madison died on June 28, 1836, at the age of 85 years old.

Montpelier was the Madison family home. James and Dolley lived there during the last twenty years of his life.

James Madison at 80 years old

Dolley and James had been married for 42 years. They had only been apart for a month or two when Dolley had a knee injury prior to his presidency. Dolley was obviously very saddened by the death of her beloved James. She spent many, many months mourning his passing. She told a friend in a letter, "Indeed I have been as one in a troubled dream since my irreparable loss of [Madison], for whom my affection was perfect, as was his character and conduct thro' life."[1]

With James gone, Dolley had to find a publisher for James's papers. James had assumed that his papers would be valued at $100,000. He based his inheritance to other family members on that figure. Dolley tried every avenue she could, but there wasn't a single publisher that would pay her that much. She was struggling financially. Her son, Payne, had made bad choices throughout his life and constantly needed her financial help. She fell deeper and deeper into debt.

She ended up selling the papers to Congress for $30,000. Since this was much lower than she had expected, she was forced to sell the Madison family home, Montpelier. In a letter to the man who purchased the home, Henry Moncure, Dolley wrote, "No one, I think can appreciate my feelings of grief and dismay at the necessity of transferring to another a beloved home."[2] But as she always did, Dolley made the best of things. She moved back to Washington and made it her permanent residence in 1844.

By this point, Dolley hadn't lived in Washington for 27 years. Things had definitely changed during her absence. Most of her friends were gone. The fashions were much different—and because of her financial situation, Dolley still wore many of her old outfits. Yet Dolley's friendly, kind personality had not—and would not—go out of style. People were fascinated by her. She had known the founders of the country! She had actually talked with and been friends with George Washington and Thomas Jefferson. She had been married to the Father of the Constitution. It didn't take Dolley long to become the belle of the ball again.

For years, people had joked that Dolley was so popular that she was a queen. And now Queen Dolley was back again! She was invited to all of the important parties. And she held plenty of them, too, at her new home across the street from the White House near Lafayette Square. She was even given an honorary seat in Congress, and whenever she visited she was allowed to sit on the main floor with the representatives. They also gave her what is called "franking" privileges. This means that she could send and receive letters through the mail without having to pay any postage. All she had to do was write her name on the upper right hand corner of the envelope in place of the stamp.

The wives of the presidents consulted her on all sorts of issues. In May 1844, Dolley was given a special honor. The first telegraph line in the world had just been constructed between Washington, D.C., and Baltimore, Maryland. Samuel F.B. Morse, the inventor of Morse Code and the telegraph, asked Dolley to be the first private citizen to send a telegram. She

Self-portrait of Samuel F.B. Morse, a painter as well as an inventor wrote to her cousin, Mrs. John Wethered, who lived in Baltimore. The telegram read, "Message from Mrs. Madison: She sends her love to Mrs. Wethered."[3]

Dolley continued to champion good causes. After the War of 1812, she funded a charity to support the orphaned children in Washington. She donated a cow so that the children would have fresh milk, gave money to help the organizers buy the supplies they needed, and even helped sew clothing for the children.[4] In 1846, at the age of 78, Dolley joined forces with Elizabeth Schuyler Hamilton (Alexander Hamilton's wife) and Louisa Catherine Johnson Adams (John Quincy Adams's wife) to help raise funds for the Washington Monument. They encouraged women around the country to hold fairs and fundraisers to earn money for the cause.

On July 4, 1848, Dolley, Elizabeth, and Louisa were seated as guests of honor at the special ceremony to lay the cornerstone of the monument. Approximately twenty thousand people came to watch the parade and hear the speeches.[5] Other important dignitaries were there that day, too, including the current president of the United States, James K. Polk, and a congressman from Illinois, Abraham Lincoln. It seemed fitting that one of Dolley's last major efforts was to help raise the money to build a monument that honored George Washington.

Dolley had enjoyed relatively good health most of her life. She lived to the age of 81—which was quite an old age for that time period. She died peacefully in her home in Washington, D.C., on July 12, 1849. Thousands attended her funeral. Both houses of Congress canceled their sessions in order to pay their respects. Ordinary citizens lined the streets to watch the procession. At her funeral, President Zachary Taylor referred to Dolley as the "first lady of the land for half a century." This was the first time a president's wife had ever been referred to as the "first lady." The title stuck.[6]

Dolley may not have been elected to a public office, but her influence was just as significant. She excelled in her role as the president's wife and was known throughout the world. She didn't have to reach that distinction by enacting important laws, by inventing some advanced piece of technology, by writing important books, or by leading a military into battle.

Thanks to Dolley Madison and other organizers, construction of the Washington Monument began in 1848. By 1854, the structure was 152 feet high.

Dolley Madison, a woman of impeccable style, was always known for her fashion sense. She was also known for her cheery disposition and the kind and gracious way she treated everyone.

She became so beloved because of her kind and gracious personality and her ability to make everyone she met feel at ease. She always made the person she was talking to feel as if they were the most important person in the room. As Henry Clay once said, "Everybody loves Mrs. Madison," to which Dolley replied, "That's because Mrs. Madison loves everybody."[7] For those reasons, and for her examples of patriotism and bravery, Dolley Payne Todd Madison will always be remembered as America's first "First Lady."

Dolley's Letter to Her Niece

This is part of a letter that Dolley wrote to her niece, Mary, in December 1831 from Montpelier.

My own dear niece,

. . . I hope you will soon be going to parties, and give me a detailed account of what is going forward amongst the various characters in Washington.

I have so long been confined by the side of my dear sick husband, never seeing or hearing outside of his room, that I make a dull correspondent.

Your uncle is better now than he was three days ago, and I trust will continue to mend, but his poor hands are still sore, and so swollen as to be almost useless, and so I lend him mine. The music-box is playing beside me, and seems well adapted to solitude as I look out at our mountains, white with snow, and the winter's wind sounding loud and cold. I hope you will take more than usual care of yourself this weather, and wish I could cover you with furs; but ah! if I dare indulge in wishes— Good night, my love.

Your fond aunt,
Dolley Madison[8]

Dolley Madison

1768 Dolley Payne is born on May 20 near Greensboro, North Carolina.

1769 The Paynes return to Virginia.

1783 John Payne frees his slaves. The Paynes move to Philadelphia. He starts a business manufacturing laundry starch.

1790 On January 7, Dolley Payne marries Quaker lawyer John Todd, Jr. in Philadelphia. Anna Payne moves in with them.

1792 On February 29, Dolley Payne Todd gives birth to her first child, John Payne Todd. Her father, John Payne, dies on October 24. Her sister, Lucy, marries George Steptoe Washington, nephew of President George Washington.

1793 William Temple Todd, Dolley's second son, is born. In October, Dolley's in-laws, husband, and infant son die in the yellow fever epidemic in Philadelphia.

1794 Dolley Payne Todd meets James Madison, a congressman from Virginia, in May. The two marry on September 15 at the home of Lucy Payne Washington. Dolley loses her membership in the Quaker religion that December.

1797 James Madison retires from the U.S. House of Representatives. The family (James, Dolley, Anna, and Payne Todd) moves to Madison's home, Montpelier, in Virginia.

1801 Thomas Jefferson appoints James Madison his secretary of state. The family moves to Washington, D.C.

1803 Dolley helps Jefferson host presidential dinners and other social functions at the White House.

1805 Dolley suffers from an ulcerated knee. She spends three and a half months in Philadelphia being treated. It is the only significant amount of time that she and James spend apart.

1809 James Madison is inaugurated fourth president of the United States and Dolley becomes Washington's first First Lady. She enlists the help of architect Benjamin Henry Latrobe and his wife, Mary Latrobe, to decorate the White House.

1812 The first wedding is held at the White House. The War of 1812 begins.

1813 James Madison is inaugurated to his second term as president of the United States.

1814 On August 24, the British burn the White House. Dolley saves the silver, official papers, the red velvet curtains, and Gilbert Stuart's portrait of George Washington.

1815 The Treaty of Ghent ends the war with Great Britain.

1817 James Madison finishes his second term. The Madisons leave Washington to retire at Montpelier.

1836 James Madison dies. Dolley tries to get James's papers privately published.

1837 The U.S. Congress offers to buy the papers for $30,000. Dolley accepts the offer.

1844 Dolley returns permanently to Washington, D.C. Congress gives her an honorary seat in Congressional Hall. She is the first private citizen to send a personal message via telegraph.

1845 Dolley officially joins the Episcopalian church, St. John's Church in Washington.

1848 Dolley serves as the Honorary Chair of a women's group to raise funds for the Washington Monument.

1849 Dolley dies on July 12. She is buried at the family graveyard at Montpelier next to James Madison.

1852 Dolley's son, Payne Todd, dies.

Chapter 1. Fire in Washington!

1. "Life, Letters, and Legacy of Dolley Payne Madison," *The Dolley Madison Project,* Letter to Sister, August 23–24, 1814, http://www2.vcdh.virginia.edu/madison/exhibit/washington/letters/082314.html

Chapter 2. Early Joys and Hardships

1. Virgil Anson Lewis, *Southern Historical Magazine: Devoted to History, Genealogy Volume 1,* p. 180.
2. The North Carolina Booklet, Great Events in North Carolina History, July–October 1919, p. 49.
3. Lucia Beverly Cutts, *Memoirs and Letters of Dolly Madison* (Cambridge, MA: Houghton Mifflin & Co, 1886), p. 4–5.
4. Ibid., p. 6.
5. Ibid., p. 10.
6. "Todd House," http://www.ushistory.org/tour/todd-house.htm
7. "John Todd House," http://www.independenceparkinstitute.com/inp/todd_house/john_todd_jr.htm
8. Samuel A. Gum, "Philadelphia Under Siege: The Yellow Fever of 1793," *The Pennsylvania Center for the Book,* Summer 2010, http://pabook.libraries.psu.edu/palitmap/YellowFever.html
9. Henry Stephens Randall, *The Life of Thomas Jefferson, Volume 2* (New York: Derby & Jackson, 1858), p. 190.

Chapter 3. Mrs. Madison

1. "John Todd House," http://www.independenceparkinstitute.com/inp/todd_house/john_todd_jr.htm
2. Lucia Beverly Cutts, *Memoirs and Letters of Dolly Madison* (Cambridge, MA: Houghton Mifflin & Co, 1886), p. 14.
3. *Historic Harewood,* 1901, p. 3. http://archive.org/streamhistoricharewood00naul/historicharewood00naul_djvu.txt
4. Ibid., p. 12.
5. Edward Lawler, Jr. "A Brief History of the President's House in Philadelphia," USHistory.org, http://www.ushistory.org/presidentshouse/history/briefhistory.htm
6. Cutts, p. 33.
7. Ibid., pp. 15–16.

Chapter 4. Life at the White House

1. "Measuring Worth" http://www.measuringworth.com/
2. "Inaugural Ball," http://www.inaugural.senate.gov/days-events/days-event/inaugural-ball
3. "To James Madison from Benjamin Henry Latrobe, 10 March 1809," National Archives Founders Online, http://founders.archives.gov/documents/Madison/03-01-02-0034
4. "Life, Letters, and Legacy of Dolley Payne Madison," *The Dolley Madison Project,* Letter to Sister, August 23–24, 1814, http://www2.vcdh.virginia.edu/madison/exhibit/washington/letters/082314.html

Chapter 5. First "First Lady"

1. "Widowhood," *James Madison's Montpelier,* http://www.montpelier.org/james-and-dolley-madison/dolley-madison/widowhood
2. "The Widowhood," "Life, Letters, and Legacy of Dolley Payne Madison," *The Dolley Madison Project,* Letter to Sister, August 23–24, 1814 http://www2.vcdh.virginia.edu/madison/overview/widow.html
3. "Widowhood," *James Madison's Montpelier.*
4. "First Ladies' Causes: Dolley's Orphanage and More," Boston.com, http://www.boston.com/news/nation/washington/articles/2010/02/08/first_ladies_causes_dolleys_orphanage_and_more/articles/2010/02/08/first_ladies_causes_dolleys_orphanage_and_more/
5. Catherine Allgor, "The Politics of Love," *Humanities, The Magazine of the National Endowment for the Humanities,* http://www.neh.gov/humanities/2010/januaryfebruary/feature/the-politics-love
6. "Dolley Madison's Biography," *James Madison's Montpelier,* http://www.montpelier.org/james-and-dolley-madison/dolley-madison/bio
7. Allgor.
8. Lucia Beverly Cutts, *Memoirs and Letters of Dolly Madison* (Cambridge, MA: Houghton Mifflin & Co, 1886), pp. 183–184.

Works Consulted

Allgor, Catherine. "The Politics of Love," *Humanities, The Magazine of the National Endowment for the Humanities,* January-February 2010, http://www.neh.gov/humanities/2010/januaryfebruary/feature/the-politics-love

Cutts, Lucia Beverly. *Memoirs and Letters of Dolly Madison.* Cambridge, MA: Houghton Mifflin & Co, 1886.

"Dolley Madison," *American Experience,* PBS, http://www.pbs.org/wgbh/americanexperience/films/dolley/

"First Ladies' Causes: Dolley's Orphanage and More," Boston.com, February 8, 2010, http://www.boston.com/news/nation/washington/articles/2010/02/08/first_ladies_causes_dolleys_orphanage_and_more

Gum, Samuel A. "Philadelphia Under Siege: The Yellow Fever of 1793," The Pennsylvania Center for the Book, Summer 2010, http://pabook.libraries.psu.edu/palitmap/YellowFever.html

Historic Harewood. Philadelphia: Washington Manor Association, 1901. http://archive.org/stream/historicharewood00naul/historicharewood00naul_djvu.txt

"Inaugural Ball," http://www.inaugural.senate.gov/days-events/days-event/inaugural-ball

"James Madison's Montpelier," http://www.montpelier.org

"John Todd House," http://www.independenceparkinstitute.com/inp/todd_house/john_todd_jr.htm

Lawler, Edward, Jr. "A Brief History of the President's House in Philadelphia," USHistory.org, http://www.ushistory.org/presidentshouse/history/briefhistory.htm

Lewis, Virgil Anson. *Southern Historical Magazine: Devoted to History, Genealogy Volume 1,* Charleston, WV: Virgil A. Lewis, 1892.

"Life, Letters, and Legacy of Dolley Payne Madison," *The Dolley Madison Project,* http://www2.vcdh.virginia.edu/madison/index.html

National First Ladies' Library, http://www.firstladies.org/biographies/firstladies.aspx?biography=4

North Carolina Booklet, Great Events in North Carolina History, July–October 1919, Raleigh, NC: Commercial Printing Company, 1919.

Randall, Henry Stephens. *The Life of Thomas Jefferson, Volume 2,* New York: Derby & Jackson, 1858.

"Todd House," http://www.ushistory.org/tour/todd-house.htm

Further Reading

Books

Brown, Don. *Dolley Madison Saves George Washington.* New York: HMH Books for Young Readers, 2007.

Kent, Zachary. *Dolley Madison: The Enemy Cannot Frighten a Free People.* Berkeley Heights, NJ: Enslow Publishers, 2010.

Krull, Kathleen. *Women Who Broke the Rules: Dolley Madison.* New York: Bloomsbury USA Children's, 2015.

Mattern, Joanne. *Dolley Madison (First Ladies).* Edina, MN: Checkerboard Library, 2007.

Smalley, Roger. *Dolley Madison Saves History (Graphic History).* Mankato, MN: Capstone Press, 2006.

On the Internet

History for Kids

    kids.usa.gov/history

National First Ladies Library

    www.firstladies.org

White House Historical Association

    www.whitehousehistory.org

The History Channel

    www.history.com

The White House

    www.whitehouse.gov

ball (ball) a fancy dance

beau (boh) a young man who is dating a young lady

belle (bell) a young lady who is at the age of dating

commandeer (kah-mun-DEER)—To officially take someone else's property for military use.

court (cort) the process of dating

inaugural (in-AW-gyur-ul) marking the beginning of a term in office for a president

Morse Code (MORS KOHD) a system of clicks and pauses, short and long sounds, or flashes of light that represent letters and numbers

representative (reh-pree-SEN-tuh-tiv) A person who is elected to Congress to vote for and make laws

spyglass (spy glass) a handheld telescope that lets a person see far away

telegram (TEL-ih-gram) a message sent by telegraph

telegraph (TEL-ih-graf) a system that sends messages over a wire by electrical signals.

Amie Jane Leavitt, a Brigham Young University graduate, is an accomplished author, researcher, and photographer. She is an adventurer who loves to travel the globe in search of interesting story ideas and beautiful places to capture in photos. She has written more than sixty books for kids, has contributed to online and print media, and has worked as a consultant, writer, and editor for numerous educational publishing and assessment companies. Amie has a deep love for U.S. history. For that reason, she particularly enjoyed researching and writing this book on Dolley Madison. To check out a listing of Amie's current projects and published works, visit her website at www.amiejaneleavitt.com.